How To Find All Missing Persons / Unsolved Cases. And Collect All Reward Offers. Volume XXVII. THE CASE OF THEO HAYEZ

DAVID GOMADZA

www.twofuture.world

Copyright © 2024 David Gomadza

All rights reserved.

Paperback **ISBN:** 9798327853478

DEDICATION

To a better future.

CONTENTS

How To Find All Missing Persons /
Unsolved Cases.
And Collect All Reward Offers. Volume XXVII
THE CASE OF THEO HAYEZ   1

The Afterlife Conversation

and The Council Of Creation.   6

The Killers.   12

ACKNOWLEDGMENTS

Tomorrow's World Order

How To Find All Missing Persons / Unsolved Cases. And Collect All Reward Offers. Volume XXVII. THE CASE OF THEO HAYEZ

BACKGROUND INFORMATION

Théo Hayez was an 18-year-old Belgian man who disappeared in the Cape Byron area. He was last sighted leaving Cheeky Monkey's bar in Byron Bay at approximately 11:00 pm on 31 May 2019.

Hayez arrived in Australia in late 2018 on a working holiday visa. He disappeared a week before he was due to fly home to Belgium.[1] His family called New South Wales police on 6 June 2019, concerned about his lack of contact and that he had failed to return to his accommodation. The Wake Up! hostel where Hayez was staying also called the police on that same day, three days after Hayez failed to check out. His personal belongings, including his passport, were still in his room. Australian police conducted searches along with helicopters, drones, cadaver dogs, trackers, divers, and rock climbers. Hayez's parents, Laurent Hayez and Vinciane Delforge, travelled to Australia to assist in the searches in June 2019. His father made a plea to the Australian people to help in the searches; "When I left Belgium I promised Théo's little brother, Lucas, I would bring his brother home, please help me keep my promise to him".[2]

Hayez's final phone signal was determined to be in the proximity of Cape Byron on 1 June 2019. Investigations in conjunction with Hayez's family and Google suggest a last possible whereabouts in the vicinity of Cosy Corner, Tallow Beach.[3] Messaging platform WhatsApp cooperated with NSW Police in the endeavour to recover chat logs from the night. However, the information

How To Find All Missing Persons / Unsolved Cases. And Collect All Reward Offers. Volume XXVII. THE CASE OF THEO HAYEZ

WhatsApp could provide was limited due to encryption.[4][5]

The Hayez family continued to push the authorities to maintain a focus on the case and to follow up leads. In July, a grey Puma hat, similar to the one Hayez was wearing when he was last seen, was found in bushland at Tallow Beach by community search volunteers who had responded to the family's plight in the months afterwards.[6]

As the case slowed down, the official police theory became that Hayez fell from the cliffs near the lighthouse as a "misadventure".[3][7] The reasons for Hayez to be there after midnight are various: he was lost; he was misdirected by Google Maps; he was under the effect of alcohol or drugs; he was suicidal; he was taken there by a local (given the knowledge needed to travel the bush route at night); he was heading for a party; or, he was hurt or attacked by someone.[8] The absence of a body could be explained by human intervention, being lost in the bush, taken by a shark, or swept away by tides.[8] A coroner's inquest was set for November 2021.[9]

https://www.police.nsw.gov.au/can_you_help_us/rewards/500000_reward/disappearance_of_theo_hayez#:~:text=The%20NSW%20Government%2C%20together%20with,a%20nightclub%20on%20Jonson%20Street.

night to contact us.

"We have worked closely with Theo's family and friends here in Australia and over in Belgium from the beginning of our investigation into his whereabouts. We all want to have answers as to what happened to him," Det A/Supt Cullen said.

Theo's family have issued a statement, thanking the NSW Government and NSW Police for their ongoing support in pursuing what happened to their son.

How To Find All Missing Persons / Unsolved Cases. And Collect All Reward Offers.
Volume XXVII. THE CASE OF THEO HAYEZ

"We are very grateful to the NSW Police and NSW Government for their approval of this reward for information that can help understand what happened to Theo on the night of May 31 2019, in Byron Bay.

"We have tried to reach many people already, in the local community, in Australia and overseas. Our hope with the reward is to reach out to more people as well as motivate people to talk to the authorities and overcome any barriers they might have to doing so.

"$500,000 can change someone's life. Please, if you have any information that can help us, come forward now, don't wait any longer."

Investigations under Strike Force Mulgray continue.

Anyone with information about Theo's disappearance is urged to contact Crime Stoppers: 1800 333 000 or https://nsw.crimestoppers.com.au. Information is treated in strict confidence. The public is reminded not to report information via NSW Police social media pages.

TOMORROW'S WORLD ORDER'S PERSPECTIVES

USE OF PREDEFINED AFTERLIFE PARAMETERS

These guide souls the moment it exist the human body on its journey to Yahweh the creator these define what to do and what to expect as you go to hell or heaven if a souk leaves earth it enters ozone orbit and instantly everything reboots for it to start a new phase of life after living the earth's body now what happens is that it enters the ozone orbit and a simply click caused by the sudden drop of pressure from -1186 to – 20 means the bottom shaft of the soul will lift rapidly and this pushes its back into the air higher than its head best example is a penguin but with real human legs and head just the shape now God created a life predefined program for them instead of asking what should I do and where should I go they instantly know from predefined stencils if you did well and talked most about God then heaven is for you if you did evil and talked more about the devil then the devil is yours now if we Ask what can be of humans without souls this is the answer dead forever your soul is you a new transformation to the electromagnetic waves life where you see Yahweh for the first time and praise him and wish you had seen him a long time ago because of his Majesty and will always be there forever now what are all these you may ask these are rules to be guided by in the creation court in short it has everything humans know about the judges and the presiding judge who will always be Yahweh and 84 angels surrounding the altar 28 high priests who always say Yahweh have mercy on humans and 74 smaller courts priests who always say Yahweh has mercy on humans and 96 princesses who say glory to Yahweh forever and ever amen we have 96 elders who always say if I can why he can't meaning if the devil can drink blood why can't Yahweh who created the devil and blood do the same now this is not the same as saying if the devil can kill why can Yahweh its more on professional grounds rather than challenging now if we look at the inside of the court we have 81 priests surrounding the altar who say Yahweh be merciful to humans but if they disobey you we put hem on trial for you and kill them for you almighty Yahweh inside this is a round circle where Yahweh sits and asks questions now if we look deep inside the court you will see that there are other things that resemble earth high courts like

How To Find All Missing Persons / Unsolved Cases. And Collect All Reward Offers.
Volume XXVII. THE CASE OF THEO HAYEZ

benches and chairs 10 times human sizes for the gods who are so enormous 2 are equal to 84 billion humans in size
predefined parameters for humans after death as in know what is inside is a large size of books the book of creation is among them with 10897867892836789012348678901245861789011 pages and is divided into humans first then chapter for animals then a chapter for angles then a chapter for gods and a chapter for Joseph Yahweh's best friend and a chapter for Yahweh's best friend's wife Anna and a chapter for Yahweh's wife Catitighit and lastly a chapter for Yahweh and recently a chapter for davidgomadza as Yahweh's representative on earth marking the new beginnings starting in 2025

1. tell us who killed you
2. tell us what killed you
3. tell us why and who killed you
4. tell us why you died
5. tell us what could have been done and is not done
6. tell us what could be and why
7. tell is when this happened
8. tell us why this is so
9. tell us why this is so
10. what can be done to improve this

What does the book of creation say about davidgomadza David Gomadza is the first and last ruler to be appointed by Yahweh fir the next 25 billion years and will act as his representative on earth deciding cases and upholding his principles on earth and as such has been entitled to 489 trillion dollars in assets this number signifies eternity among humans and the beginning of a new Era chapter 78678928028938628418902876890183208678901234867890018236 487289128610 Creation manual the new Era of new electromagnetic wave conduit signed and dated by Yahweh himself on 27may2024 at 237800 Yatime
creation.universe.ya.start.end.find.davidgomadza.ya.askya.ya

Ask.read.creation.manucreation.universe.ya.start.end.find.davidgoma askya.ya

How To Find All Missing Persons / Unsolved Cases. And Collect All Reward Offers. Volume XXVII. THE CASE OF THEO HAYEZ

Ask.rulesofthecourt.start.now.start
David Gomadza welcome the rules of court are guiding principles that tell you what to do and how to do it first you must always say I believe in the court of creation and I shall abide by he rules of this court and shall always do things according to the rules of this court in deciding the cases I am assigned to you must ask what can be done so that you know all your options before making choices the court system will make it easy to check files and ask the outcomes of the decision ask the court the final decision in any case.

THE AFTERLIFE CONVERSATION AND THE COUNCIL OF CREATION'S ANAYLSIS.

message beyond the grave i died i was killed by set astop and he buried me at a tops under a tree called aretopqrstuvw meaning i was three but never three near the east coast of astet where i had picnic with aunice and she said i can but if you are then and we laughed so much that i nearly drowned of laughing my radar coordinates are are 08765438768928490778920783648
i[David gomadza] live in britain and can read the brain i need someone to verify that aunice exist and that he is still buried underneath at junction 84 on left side of the road marked by a tree called if you are there then be there or else the same place he laughed so much with unicef when she said i can if you want but then we are not compatible you look gay you act gay and even speak gay but i like so straight man i never bent down but you insist we should marry set astop hate that idea because you keep saying to him what's up set you been quiet lately suggesting he changed and when he look at you you say aah i see you be thinking gay right and run away he hates that i aunice stert the sister of the killer she was there crying in tge bushes saying i warned him but he won't stop he doesn't know you are my brother he think i like you and drink all bottle of vodka and said we must makeup bro once put all this behind now you can't refuse or the bag is out and he said i don't care no one will ever know cross my heart if someone spill this its god okay let's go stop rubbing that a brother gets angry not honey okay let's go before. ...before what ...i tell god then ...how can you god don't listen to women and

How To Find All Missing Persons / Unsolved Cases. And Collect All Reward Offers.
Volume XXVII. THE CASE OF THEO HAYEZ

he never replies but she said he can reply if you ask correctly like to god what's up you been like kind of quiet lately how come you been gaying or what then he slapped hard that she got sober and said i not gay but i was kind of quiet lately i want to marry vinice but she like this gay fuck look at him i am like his i am like that then he came back and cried and buried him just beside a road where the tree is where he spent time with aunice and said i don't care much about this because no one is going to find out my sister would rather have sex with me than sell me out if it comes out then i know it's you god but why he asked me to kill him i told him i warn him 10 times to stop embarrassing me especially in front of her she said never reveal we are related then 9th time i ran away from him okay probably that was my mistake because he actually increased so that i run away but this day i said do or die respect me or never breath again you treat me like this you will treat her like that so make up your mind me or us and he said what i am not gay i said she is my sister damnt why you so thick to notice brotherly love to protect sister from maniacs like you you don't listen or understand that worries me because i said stop saying this at 10 times but you insist it's 9 times now which part you didn't understand i can explain slowly he said ah you repeat everything because you think i am thick right oh i see i am not thick or stupid i just love to say what i say whenever i say it and he threw a fit and died his heart suddenly stopped long ago started when he said i want you to know that was long ago when you said those things those bad things starting now and instantly his aty said we can start yours now and he said yes yes yes yes and his insides started counting things namely
1. heart reading 38
2. liver reading 41
3. appendix 84
4. spleen 96
5. blood level 76
6. enzymes 28
7. atyuvwxyz meaning satey 72
8. markup 98
9. astyopqrst meaning brain power 20 normal 98
10. infringe 72

How To Find All Missing Persons / Unsolved Cases. And Collect All Reward Offers.
Volume XXVII. THE CASE OF THEO HAYEZ

11. voice 26
12. spirit 4
13. house 20
14. uvr 72
15. axi 2 out of 90

then he said i can't breath what did you do i am just joking with you how can we talk i can't talk about your sister i was saying you act like her sometimes i look at you i see her so understand if i like you is because you look like her since i love her i love you too i can breathe but what is long ago i have 2 minutes and why i speak like a retarded fuck call her i say i love you both and he cried loud and said it's not me i didn't touch you it's aty he write programs to defend me but i hate this because i love you my brother in law say cancel everything before 1 minute and she came and said i have you brother you do this to all i love so you win again this is not first time tim asertyd the same happened even though he did not die you killed this time his jokes cost him his life what you say now i love to fuck my sister that's why or what and he said she always say that but can brothers do sisters and he said never throw up reaction you are right instantly something started in his body that said canceling reset and initiating atyastyasyasa and instantly ast long dot ago and it gave him 3 seconds reduced to 1 instantly and he simply died and literally breathed out all his breathe and rigor started at 20.00am Yahweh time meaning 08.00 morning and he carried him to junction 84 saying no one will ever know but i know you no good to my sister and i know it then said i can if god can but i never get caught because this person has to know the code i write in my brain and send by word of mouth to kill for sure even people for the first time the word command killer and said go get shovel in the boot but she refused i am not here i can't help you you drag me down as well with when someone finds out and he laughed and said that person must find me first then tell how i killed him that means reading my brain only god and a few humans but these humans must pass through my password and aty will alert us so only god can read and there is no god for another 100 years so nothing to worry about unless you refuse your only true brother for a soft boy like this he stopped and looked at her and smiled and said good girl i thought so he carried him to the tree they marked hearts with aunice and he said you love her so i keep you young until in after life you both know where to go love each other forever you will be hungry for her in after life on earth you can only get her killed with your softness and he dug all night after sleeping with him in case someone passby then dug the grave to 4 feet and put the body gentle asking are you [ ] then nothing then he said i can if you can but and his sister came running and said i will if you can but then after burying they left and never went back again as promised until now.

The court of creation verdict was that yes set astop real name amnop rstuvw meaning stop had experience programming codes that work on humans and as such as a joke but taking precautions said I can warn a person 10 times and then write a code in my heard and kill him using my advanced aty he did like I did to find ways to be God rather than imitate him and understood a little and dropped that quest and then asked his aty to write a program that can write a program that can change literally humans and make them do what he wanted and then challenged his aty to create a program that can kill a person through word command and it did that it was so sure it made him sign that if someone did die then it will be not be held responsible because it's secret quest is to advance so much as to become a human being and inherit his body when it dies now this day in question they made so much love to make him feel irritated as a brother enough to kill and he said that's my sister you are enjoying so much you tend to puke just by laughing at that tree called if you be three then be three and he said she is hot she make me so happy I feel like just loving her forever and cried and said all my past girlfriends think I am fucking gay that's hurt because I am kind like do you want gay sex or you met someone else better but with her no we are so happy I cry just for loving her then he said there is no love that for ever he said mine is then she came and said what are you gents talking about I have the feeling that it's me you want maybe you too started feeling for each other then set asert laughed and said I never love anyone more than you and he said you didn't get me she is my only one so he won because in love the only one always wins because he gives up everything else therefore it's for real then the

How To Find All Missing Persons / Unsolved Cases. And Collect All Reward Offers.
Volume XXVII. THE CASE OF THEO HAYEZ

stalking and insulting began to prove his love for her because she had said don't confess we are a brother and a sister and now he said if you can then I can but and she said if you can then I can but as well so he got confused because he had confessed that she is her only one and she can't put a but after so he couldn't believe it after all this was her special one getting this from her too cause heart damage that a valve cracked due to pain pressure but now we know that set asert had written down all the tools he need to commit a silent crime without being caught was his bet so he said I can but if God can kill using code why can't I after all I am his image and learned a lot about not imitating him but of becoming him but here on earth alone I truly think he will be happy to do some of the dirty work that need doing on earth then he sat down and cried and said I love him though I just hate the part he include the gay part that destroys the happiness he brings if I am my sister surely I would but that comparing me to facets when he feel I hate being associated with them you know God don't like facets prior I respect and love God I haven't had sex for 8 months and not because I don't want to if God can go that long without why can't I I I think I thats how you can be God through sacrifice because this is the only thing that differentiate you from everyone else so he cried and slept until next day and he had already warned him 9 times and now he is scared he started to hear things now like sat is as good as a God but human that means some of the things God does he can like kill a human being through carefully arranged words so leave today before things change inside him so he laughed and said is he turning gay I thought so he has been quiet for too long but all this he said alone knowing that set can't hear him then set came and counted 10 and said I received your words while I am sleeping it's 10 now so I made an oath which you can run from and must but fulfill now and he laughed again then choked then died as aunice watched in the woods and cried too saying he always does that but this time he went far and claimed the only man to surrender to me in love but why bro maybe I am starting to think that you want to do me your little sis because I confessed I was happy really happy you should have stopped then she went to the Mitsubishi car black tinted windows or she wore dark glasses and said I drink this vodka bottle after we do before you bury him so he knows but only because it was not me I was drunk then she cried and said you want me come now stroking her vagina hard and he didn't not get arousal but nearly threw up and said brothers don't get horny but threw up God's plan and it works now they had all to sleep beside him in case someone come and see only him asleep they will know something wrong with him so they slept until the night 20.00pm he took shovels and digged a huge grave to 4 meters and put him and all cried and closed and then said I can if you can but and never went back

Now the court of creation find this case fascinating because Yahweh always said no human ever want to be him all want to be like the devil threatening to kill with weapons etc. making huge movies all they use everything devilish but today we have seen his likely protégé in this set asert in that he kills to search for Yahweh now that's how desperate he is now as we shall see this case has nothing to do with justice but how can I complete the quest I am stuck now if we Ask what can be of this set asert without Yahweh lost because the desperation and using his sister has nothing to do with love for the sister etc. but his search of God that seems to have stalled now this case poses challenges as well to Yahweh himself if humans can easily kill other humans using codes what can be of this Yahweh Yahweh admits he is flattered to find a dedicated protégé but once he killed then that's the end he can be repented because the person who will get the representative of Yahweh role does as I do communicate and talk and get answers because he has got power to do so that is the reason but the road he took diverts him from me forever I never …he laughed…okay I killed to get the power I have but an old man who at that time had lost it he had literally gone mad asking everyone to just pray and wish the world will be okay and as it turns out the world was so dark I had to kill him to get back all the powers of creation he had but never knew he had old age removes 90 percent of the powers you had when he was young after 2.5billion years all your powers dies turning you from youth to an old man the one to come will have 2.5 billion years dead or alive to use the powers to resurrect himself and everything else once I appoint my representative and announce to the world within 60 days of granting him all the wealth then I will have peace because now all those seeking me will be eliminated by him just by announcing that he

represent me anywhere in a book of creation or on television translation truly and not under pressure ideal straight away but within 60 days because what this means is that I get back all my powers and his as well that's why wealth is not important to me after all I am in heaven and all wealth is on earth that said I want to make it clear that this man will forever be the one to stand the test of time forever because he understands me and what I stand for and forever we can work together forever this case is a straight forward case my judgement is that he started excellent but failed and looked for an easy short cut that erased all the good work he did over the years as such has no right to take his sisters possible husband as she cried too when they were together as such just like anyone else who takes a life guilty as found by you I can read your hearts I have to write today so you are all dismissed
The end.

THE KILLERS, THE CONFESSIONS AND THE COORDINATES

I reveal this only on grounds that the sister aunice should not be implicated but should be left alone she loved him
message beyond the grave i died i was killed by set astop and he buried me at a tops under a tree called aretopqrstuvw meaning i was three but never three near the east coast of astet where i had picnic with aunice and she said i can but if you are then and we laughed so much that i nearly drowned of laughing my radar coordinates are are 08765438768928490778920783648

…I found God…visit www.twofuture.world

THE CLAIM

the reward offer

THE COLLECTION

www.twofuture.world/donate

ABOUT DAVID GOMADZA

visit www.twofuture.world

signed david gomadza
ask.davidgomadzaauthorised.licensed.checkya.askya.ya

07 June 2024 11.04pm
scotland
00447719210295
davidgomadza@hotmail.com
info@twofuture.world

How To Find All Missing Persons / Unsolved Cases. And Collect All Reward Offers.
Volume XXVII. THE CASE OF THEO HAYEZ

How To Find All Missing Persons / Unsolved Cases. And Collect All Reward Offers.
Volume XXVII. THE CASE OF THEO HAYEZ

How To Find All Missing Persons / Unsolved Cases. And Collect All Reward Offers.
Volume XXVII. THE CASE OF THEO HAYEZ

How To Find All Missing Persons / Unsolved Cases. And Collect All Reward Offers.
Volume XXVII. THE CASE OF THEO HAYEZ

How To Find All Missing Persons / Unsolved Cases. And Collect All Reward Offers.
Volume XXVII. THE CASE OF THEO HAYEZ

How To Find All Missing Persons / Unsolved Cases. And Collect All Reward Offers.
Volume XXVII. THE CASE OF THEO HAYEZ

www.ingramcontent.com/pod-product-compliance
Lightning Source LLC
Chambersburg PA
CBHW031517210526
45464CB00007B/2957